BY KAY
BARNHAM

WAYLAND

First published in 2013 by Wayland
Copyright © Wayland 2013

Wayland
338 Euston Road
London NW1 3BH

Wayland Australia
Level 17/207 Kent Street
Sydney, NSW 2000

Commissioning editor: Debbie Foy
Designer: Lisa Peacock
Series editor: Camilla Lloyd

Dewey ref: 782.4'2164'0922-dc23
ISBN: 978 0 7502 7932 1
10 9 8 7 6 5 4 3 2 1

Printed in UK
Wayland is a division of Hachette Children's Books,
an Hachette UK company

www.hachette.co.uk

The author and publisher would like to thank the following for allowing their
pictures to be reproduced in this publication: Cover FilmMagic/Getty Images;
4 © Rune Hellestad/Corbis; 8 © Splash News/Corbis; 10 © Nancy Kaszerman/
ZUMA Press/Corbis; 16 © James Whatling/Splash/Splash News/Corbis; 22 © Sayre
Berman/Corbis; 28 © John A.Angelillo/Corbis; 34 © Ron Smits/London Ent/Splash
News/Corbis; 49 © Splash News/Corbis; 67 © Comic Relief/Splash News/Corbis;
82 © PAUL MILLER/epa/Corbis.

One Direction is the registered trademark of 1D Media Limited
This book is not affiliated with or endorsed by One Direction or any of their
publishers or licensees.

Want to know EVERYTHING there is to know about

ONE DIRECTION?

Then head this way...

SINCE THEY HIT THE BIG TIME ON
The X Factor IN 2010, THEY HAVE BECOME THE
BIGGEST BOY BAND ON THE PLANET. THEY ARE NIALL
HORAN, ZAYN MALIK, LIAM PAYNE, HARRY STYLES
AND LOUIS TOMLINSON. **They are...**

ONE DIRECTION!

Niall Harry Zayn Louis Liam

But do you know everything there is to know about your idols? Can you sing along with every single track they've ever recorded? How tall are they? Who thought of the band's name? Who's afraid of spoons?

This book tells you **EVERYTHING** you need to know about One Direction. Right now, you're just a few pages away from becoming one of the greatest Directioners **EVER**. But there's more. Armed with your new stack of facts, you'll also get to prove your **über-fan status** by scoring top marks in the fiendishly difficult quizzes dotted throughout the book.

WANT TO KNOW YOUR IDOLS?

Then there's only ONE DIRECTION to go...

In 2010, five solo singers named Niall, Zayn, Liam, Harry and Louis entered the boys' category of the UK's **The X Factor**. They all wanted to win. This was their chance to become stars and win the biggest talent show on television.

THEN DISASTER STRUCK.

They didn't get through!

But guest judge **Nicole Scherzinger** of the Pussycat Dolls stepped in. Maybe, she said, the five boys were not meant to sing alone. Maybe, they were meant to sing together. **Simon Cowell**, one of the biggest names in the music industry, agreed. So they tried it – and Nicole was right. Together, the boys were pure **MAGIC**.

Who thought of the band's name? That was Harry. He figured that there was only **one direction** he and the others should be heading – towards winning **The X Factor**.

BUT DISASTER STRUCK AGAIN.

MATT CARDLE WON **THE X FACTOR.**

REBECCA FERGUSON CAME SECOND.

AND ONE DIRECTION CAME THIRD.

Was ONE DIRECTION's dream over...?

NO. If anything, their dream was just beginning. After **The X Factor** final, it was revealed that thanks to Simon Cowell, One Direction had a record deal with Sony Music label **Syco Music**.

ONE DIRECTION were on the way UP.

7

'When they sing, they enjoy what they're doing. They put their heart and soul in it. And they love their fans. They are so down to earth and no one can ever say fame has changed them.'

– Shreya, 14

Do you remember what
the boys sang at their solo
auditions on **The X Factor**,
BEFORE forming One
Direction?

Check out the cryptic clues
to remind yourself...

1. Niall must have felt very poorly when he sang this.

2. Zayn's track rhymed with 'Vet Tree Dove Goo'.

3. Poor Liam shed so many tears singing this that he could have filled the Mississippi.

4. Ah, isn't he lovely? It's no wonder that Harry made it big after singing this track.

5. If you've ever heard Tom Jones's famous song about a woman, you'll recognise her name in Louis's song too.

All answers on
pages 88-93

NIALL HORAN

The Cute One

Full name: Niall James Horan

Date of birth: 13 September 1993

Place of birth: Mullingar, County Westmeath, Ireland

Height: 171 cm (5 feet 7 inches)

Eye colour: Blue

Hair colour: Blond

Favourite colour: Blue

Nickname: Nialler

Twitter name: @NiallOfficial

- Niall has played the **guitar** for years.

- He has an older brother called Greg.

- He starred in a school play of **Oliver Twist** when he was 10 years old.

- Before appearing on **The X Factor**, he toured Ireland as a support act for Lloyd Daniels, who took part in **The X Factor** 2009.

- He entertained other hopefuls queuing for **The X Factor** auditions by singing **Justin Bieber's One Time** and accompanying himself on guitar.

IN JANUARY 2011, HARRY, LIAM,
LOUIS, NIALL AND ZAYN FLEW TO
LOS ANGELES FOR A FEW DAYS.
YAY. SUN-KISSED BEACHES. SUNSET
BOULEVARD. RODEO DRIVE, BABY!

ER, NO.

One Direction weren't jetting off to the **showbiz**
capital of the USA for a post-competition holiday and
a spending spree. They were going to start recording
their debut album in a **swanky LA** recording studio.
(Don't worry, though. The weather was fabulous,
they had a pool to chill beside and they did squeeze in
a spot of shopping, so it wasn't ALL hard work.)

By the time the band arrived back at Heathrow
Airport in the UK, **One Direction fever** had hit
and a crowd of hysterical fans were there to
meet them. The boys were mobbed and had to
be rescued **IN A POLICE VAN!**

And it was still only January!

The rest of the year was a WHIRLWIND of music, touring and chart-topping hits.

The X Factor 2011 Live Tour was a huge success and One Direction's first experience of a nationwide tour. They performed for an eye-popping 500,000 fans. That's half a million. That's **A LOT** of people.

In September 2011, their debut single – **What Makes You Beautiful** – shot straight to the top of the UK singles' chart. And if that wasn't enough, **Up All Night** became the fastest-selling debut album in the UK in 2011. It was official. **One Direction had conquered the UK.**

What was next...?

The rest of the world, that's what.

In **2012**, only two public figures appeared on Facebook more times than **One Direction**.

They were the candidates taking part in the US Presidential Election – **Barack Obama** (whose daughter Malia just happens to be one of **One Direction**'s biggest fans) and Mitt Romney.

by @Louis__Tomlinson

The biggest thank you possible in 140 characters to everyone worldwide who has bought our album and single. You inspire us!

So good to be back in Paris!!! C'est fantastique!

I've bruised my big toe.

Buzzzinnggggggggg

ZAYN MALIK

The Vain One

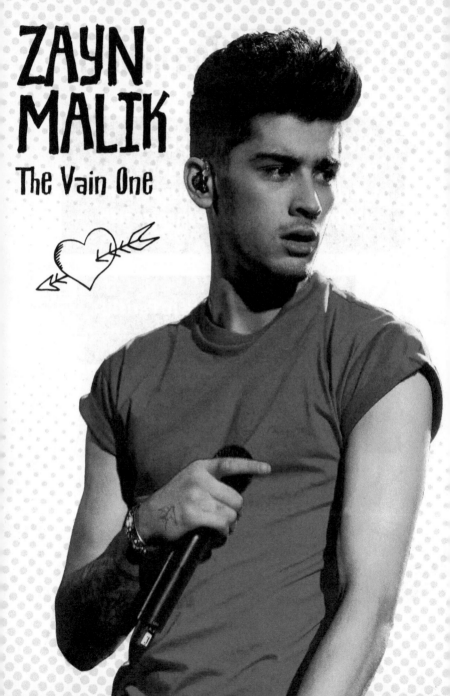

Full name: Zayn Javadd Malik

Date of birth: 12 January 1993

Place of birth: Bradford, England

Height: 175 cm (5 feet 9 inches)

Eye colour: Brown

Hair colour: Black

Favourite colour: Red

Nickname: Zaynster

Twitter name: @zaynmalik

- Zayn's dad is called **Yaser**. His mum's called **Tricia**.

- He has three sisters. **Doniya** is older than Zayn. **Waliyha** and **Safaa** are younger.

- His name used to be spelled 'Zain', but he thought it looked better with a Y.

- He can play the **triangle**.

- Before appearing on **The X Factor**, Zayn had never travelled out of the UK. He didn't even have his own passport.

✩ ✩ ✩ STAR SIGNS ✩ ✩ ✩

Some people believe that
your date of birth determines
who you get along with! Are you
and the boys well matched?

ZAYN's birthday is
12 January 1993, so he's
a **Capricorn**. You'll get
on well with him if
you're Taurus or Virgo.
But if you're Scorpio
or Pisces, you're
well matched, too.

HARRY is the youngest.
His birthday is **1 February
1994** and he's an
Aquarius. According to
the stars, he's supposed
to be best mates with
Gemini and Libra and
good mates with Aries
and Saggitarius.

NIALL was born on **13 September 1993**, which means that he's a **Virgo**. Gets on best with Taurus and Capricorn, but he has a soft spot for Cancer and Scorpio, too.

LOUIS arrived on **Christmas Eve 1991**, which makes him the second **Capricorn** of the band. He too gets along with Taurus, Virgo, Scorpio and Pisces. But there's a chance for Gemini and Leo, too.

LIAM has been around since **29 August 1993**. He's a **Virgo** too, so like Niall he gets along with Taurus and Capricorn. Leo and Libra, you might also be friends with him.

THE ONE DIRECTION
WORLD TOUR

One Direction played in all these venues!

London • Glasgow • Cardiff • Dublin

• Belfast • Manchester • Liverpool •

Sheffield • Nottingham • Birmingham •

Newcastle • Paris • Amnéville • Antwerp

• Amsterdam • Oberhausen • Herning

• Baerum • Stockholm • Copenhagen

• Berlin • Hamburg • Zurich • Munich

• Verona • Milan • Barcelona •

Madrid • Lisbon • Mexico City • Sunrise •
Miami • Louisville • Columbus • Nashville
• Atlanta • Raleigh • Washington DC •
Philadelphia • Mansfield • Wantagh •
East Rutherford • Montreal • Hershey •
Pittsburgh • Toronto • Auburn Hills • Tinley
Park • Minneapolis • Kansas City • Houston
• Dallas • Denver • West Valley City •
Vancouver • Seattle • San Jose • Oakland • Las
Vegas • Chula Vista • Los Angeles • Adelaide •
Perth • Melbourne • Sydney • Christchurch
• Auckland • Brisbane

If you were one of the lucky ones to get tickets, where did YOU see your idols?

LIAM PAYNE

The Sensible One

Full name: Liam James Payne

Date of birth: 29 August 1993

Place of birth: Wolverhampton, England

Height: 178 cm (5 feet 10 inches)

Eye colour: Brown

Hair colour: Brown

Favourite colour: Purple

Nickname: Liamp/Liamo

Twitter name: @Real_Liam_Payne

- His two older sisters are called **Ruth** and **Nicola**.

- One of Liam's kidneys stopped working when he was very young, which has meant he's had a lot of health problems. Then in 2012, he had some truly **amazing** news – during a hospital check-up, it was discovered that both of his kidneys were now working normally! He announced the good news to his fans on **Twitter**.

- He's a **boxer**.

- He plays the **guitar**.

- His two pet turtles are called **Boris** and **Archimedes**.

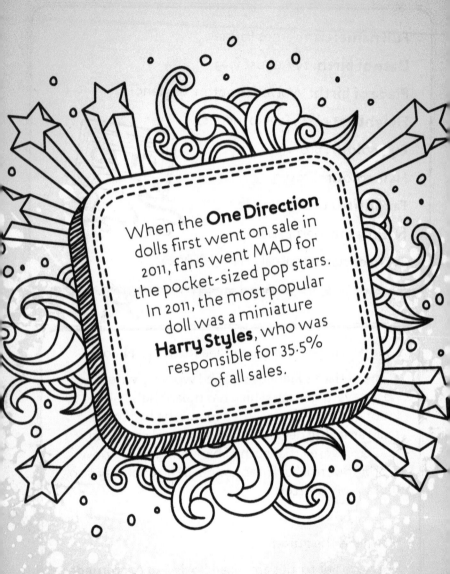

When the **One Direction** dolls first went on sale in 2011, fans went MAD for the pocket-sized pop stars. In 2011, the most popular doll was a miniature **Harry Styles**, who was responsible for 35.5% of all sales.

☆ ☆ ☆ WHO'S WHO? ☆ ☆ ☆

UNSCRAMBLE THE LETTERS TO
FIND THE NAMES OF ALL THE MEMBERS
OF YOUR FAVOURITE BOY BAND. THAT'S
INCLUDING THEIR MIDDLE NAMES,
TO MAKE IT **SUPER** TRICKY...

EARL JOHN ANIMALS

★★★★★

JAVA LADY ADZ MINK

★★★★★

MAILMAN SAY JEEP

★★★★★

DASTARDLY SHREW RYE

★★★★★

ILLUMINATION LIMO SLOWS

All answers on pages 88-93

ONE THING THAT MOST NON-AMERICAN BANDS NEVER MANAGE TO DO IS BREAK AMERICA. (DON'T WORRY. THIS ISN'T AT ALL VIOLENT. IT JUST MEANS BEING SUCCESSFUL THERE.) IT'S A NOTORIOUSLY DIFFICULT THING TO DO. A FEW BANDS HAVE MANAGED IT, LIKE THE BEATLES, THE ROLLING STONES AND COLDPLAY, BUT IN 2012, ONE MORE UK BAND WAS ADDED TO THE LIST. WHO WERE THEY…?

ONE DIRECTION, of course.

Their debut album was the first album by a UK-Irish group to go straight to number one in the US charts. And when **One Direction** toured North America in 2012, their fans went **WILD**.

- Hundreds of fans camped outside Radio City Music Hall in **New York City**.

★★★★★

- In a **Boston** mall, the band was mobbed.

★★★★★

- The police were called when fans surrounded the band's **Toronto** hotel.

★★★★★

And when One Direction took part in a live webchat, an astounding 23,000 fans signed up to take part. (That's **TWENTY-THREE THOUSAND** fans, which is the population of a small town. And they were all online talking to One Direction, **AT THE SAME TIME**. Totally amazing.)

One Direction have officially made it in the **USA**. And to prove it, at the end of 2012 they played one of the most popular venues in **New York City** to a sell-out audience.

Turn to pages 32-33 to find out more...

HARRY STYLES

The Funny One

Full name: Harry Edward Styles

Date of birth: 1 February 1994

Place of birth: Holmes Chapel, Cheshire, England

Height: 180 cm (5 feet 11 inches)

Eye colour: Green

Hair colour: Brown

Favourite colour: Orange

Nickname: Hazza or H

Twitter name: @Harry__Styles

- He can play the **kazoo**.

- He used to work in a **bakery** in Cheshire. When he goes home, he always pops into the bakery to visit his old workmates.

- He supports **Manchester United**.

- He can **juggle**.

- He'd love to be able to travel through time.

- In 2012, the most popular boy's name in the entire UK was … **Harry**. Coincidence? Nah.

by @Real_Liam_Payne

I'd just like to say a big thank you to the man/woman who made twister ice creams – you're gangster from liam payne and zayn malik

Ohh i wish i could follow all of you at once but twitter wont let me, be back to follow more soonnnn ! :)

I just had monster munch and 2 milky bars for breakfast

Nananananana batmannnn

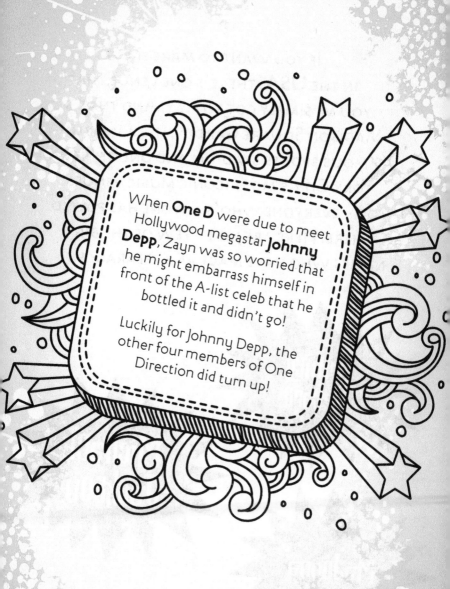

When **One D** were due to meet Hollywood megastar **Johnny Depp**, Zayn was so worried that he might embarrass himself in front of the A-list celeb that he bottled it and didn't go!

Luckily for Johnny Depp, the other four members of One Direction did turn up!

IF YOU WANT TO MAKE IT BIG IN THE **USA**, THERE'S ONE VENUE THAT YOU'VE SIMPLY GOT TO PLAY. AND THAT'S MADISON SQUARE GARDEN. IT'S A WORLD-FAMOUS SPORTS STADIUM AND ONE OF NEW YORK CITY'S MOST ICONIC MUSIC VENUES TOO – EVERYONE WHO'S ANYONE HAS PLAYED HERE. HERE ARE JUST A FEW OF THE BIG NAMES WHO HAVE MADE AN APPEARANCE...

Britney Spears

Michael Jackson

Madonna

Justin Bieber

Lady Gaga

Elvis Presley

After **One Direction** announced that they were playing Madison Square Garden in December 2012, fans went **MAD**. And not just US fans. People travelled from all over the world to come and see the boys perform. Although first they had to get a ticket and that wasn't easy – 20,000 tickets sold out **IN UNDER A MINUTE**.

THE GIG WAS A TRIUMPH.

TICKETS

LOUIS TOMLINSON

The Leader

Full name: Louis William Tomlinson

Date of birth: 24 December 1991

Place of birth: Doncaster, South Yorkshire, England

Height: 175 cm (5 feet 9 inches)

Eye colour: Blue

Hair colour: Brown

Favourite colour: Red

Nickname: Lou or Boo Bear

Twitter name: @Louis_Tomlinson

• He has five younger sisters called **Phoebe**, **Daisy**, **Félicité**, **Lottie** and **Georgia**.

• His idol is Robbie Williams. When the band sang with him on **The X Factor** it was a dream come true for Louis.

• He was Danny Zuko in his school's production of **Grease** – the role made famous by John Travolta.

• His least favourite food in the whole wide world is baked beans.

• His favourite food is Marmite. Wow!

by @Harry_Styles

Thinking about what we were doing three years ago... Today we play Madison Square Garden. We can never say thank you enough. **We love you .xx**

Snooze strikes again.

Today, I met The Queen.

Since using twitter, I find I try to use the shortest sentences possible. All the time. Sometimes you need 141 characters.

✰ ✰ ✰ SPOT THE SLOGAN ✰ ✰ ✰

ONE DIRECTION
HAVE A VERY FAMOUS
SLOGAN. CAN YOU
SPOT IT BELOW?

1. One band. One direction. One dream.

2. One band. One dream. One direction.

3. One band. One hope. One dimension.

4. One band. Five heartthrobs. One direction.

5. One candy. One ice cream. One confection.

All answers on pages 88-93

 **By @lzaynmalik**

Can't get over you guys. Don't get how much you amaze me. Thank you for everything, you truly are the best fans in the world. Love you all x

Let's hear it for NEW YORK :) goodnight everyone x

Having a great time at the royal variety show !! :D

 YAWN!

'I am CRAZY! CRAZY! CRAZY! about you guys. I think that I am your number ONE FAN!!! You guys are amazing singers and I love love love <3 you so much. :-) :-)

PS If I meet you or you meet me it will make my life. I LOVE YOU ONE DIRECTION. XXX XX YOU ARE THE BEST.'

Olivia, 12

'I'VE NEVER SEEN A BAND CAUSE SO MUCH HYSTERIA SO EARLY IN THEIR CAREER!'

LOUIS WALSH ON THE X FACTOR

'THIS IS THE FIRST TIME IN ALL THE YEARS OF THE X FACTOR WHEN I GENUINELY BELIEVE A GROUP IS GONNA WIN THIS COMPETITION.'

Simon Cowell on The X Factor.
(He was actually wrong about that, because One Direction came third. But they have since become one of the biggest boy bands in the world, so he was sort of right because they won something much bigger – worldwide fame!)

'You're my guilty pleasure!'
Cheryl Cole on The X Factor

'You are a boy band doing exactly what a boy band should do!'
Dannii Minogue on The X Factor

☆ ☆ ☆ THE MEGAMIX QUIZ ☆ ☆ ☆

Unmix the letters of these 10 bizarre song titles to find the totally famous One Direction hits hidden there!

UNLOVELIER WEIGH YEW

FAT RISKS LISTS

GONE THIN

NAP HUG TILL

HAMLET OYSTER

TOGA BUY TOE

HAIRNET MOTHS

THE TING TILLS

CAMP BED NOISY ROO

ARENA HERO NOW TOY

43

All answers on pages 88-93

♡ by @NiallOfficial

Chillin havin a laugh!
Great craic ! Family and friends!
That's what's up!

Another day in Tokyo ! Love this place!

What a sick day in the studio!
Got loads of vocal down and
recorded 2 songs! On guitar!
#worldtour2013 #cantwait

When I go home, it's like I never left! That town is class! Love Mullingar!

✦ ✦ ✦ WHO'S WHO? ✦ ✦ ✦

While recording their video diaries on **The X Factor**, the boys gave each other nicknames. But do you know which name BELONGS to which band member...?

THE VAIN ONE

★★★★★

THE SENSIBLE ONE

★★★★★

THE LEADER

★★★★★

THE CUTE ONE

★★★★★

THE FUNNY ONE

45

All answers on pages 88-93

MUSICAL INFLUENCES

Each member of One Direction has their own totally unique taste in music. Check out their favourite bands, songs, albums, idols and their very first concerts and find out which one of them you are most like...

Louis

FAVOURITE BANDS: The Fray; The Killers

FAVOURITE SONG: 'Look After You' by The Fray

FAVOURITE ALBUM: 'How to Save a Life' by The Fray

BIGGEST IDOL: Robbie Williams

FIRST CONCERT: Busted

Harry

FAVOURITE BANDS: The Beatles; Queen; Coldplay;
The Lumineers

FAVOURITE SONG: 'Shine On You Crazy Diamond' by
Pink Floyd

FAVOURITE ALBUM: '21' by Adele

BIGGEST IDOL: Chris Martin (Coldplay)

FIRST CONCERT: Nickelback

Liam

FAVOURITE BAND: One Republic

FAVOURITE SONG: 'Happy Birthday To You'

FAVOURITE ALBUM: 'Echo' by Leona Lewis

BIGGEST IDOLS: Take That

FIRST CONCERT: Gareth Gates

Niall

FAVOURITE BANDS: The Script; The Coronas.

FAVOURITE SONGS: 'Viva La Vida' by Coldplay;
'Fly Me to the Moon' by Frank Sinatra.

FAVOURITE ALBUM: 'Crazy Love' by Michael Bublé.

BIGGEST IDOLS: McFly

FIRST CONCERT: Busted

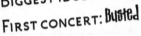

Zayn

FAVOURITE BAND: *NSYNC

FAVOURITE SONG: 'Thriller' by Michael Jackson

FAVOURITE ALBUM: 'Anything' by Donell Jones

BIGGEST IDOL: Pink

FIRST CONCERT: JLS

Liam has a **phobia about spoons**. But don't worry – he's not going to starve. He's fine with all other types of cutlery. (Though a waitress once told him off for using a fork to eat soup in a restaurant.)

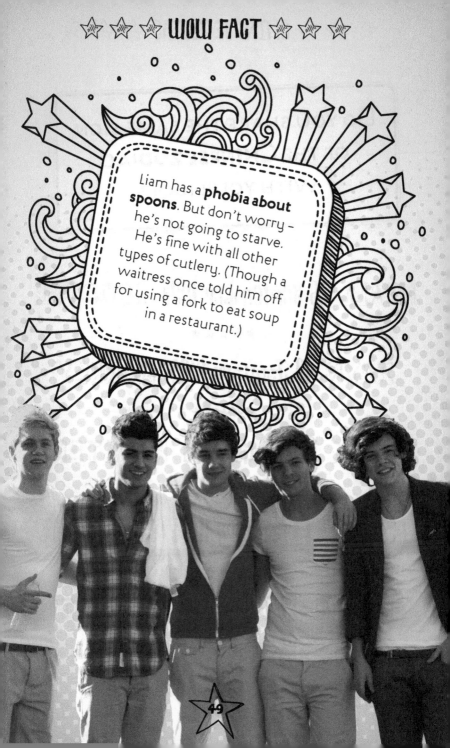

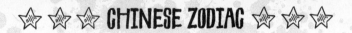
DO YOU SHARE THE SAME SIGN
OF THE **CHINESE ZODIAC**
WITH YOUR IDOL?

NIALL 13 September 1993 ROOSTER

★★★★★

ZAYN 12 January 1993 MONKEY

★★★★★

LIAM 29 August 1993 ROOSTER

★★★★★

HARRY 1 February 1994 ROOSTER

★★★★★

LOUIS 24 December 1991 GOAT

Find your date of birth here to find which sign of the Chinese Zodiac you are.

8 February 1997 – 27 January 1998	**OX**
28 January 1998 – 15 February 1999	**TIGER**
16 February 1999 – 4 February 2000	**RABBIT**
5 February 2000 – 23 January 2001	**DRAGON**
24 January 2001 – 11 February 2002	**SNAKE**
12 February 2002 – 31 January 2003	**HORSE**
1 February 2003 – 21 January 2004	**GOAT**
22 January 2004 – 8 February 2005	**MONKEY**
9 February 2005 – 28 January 2006	**ROOSTER**

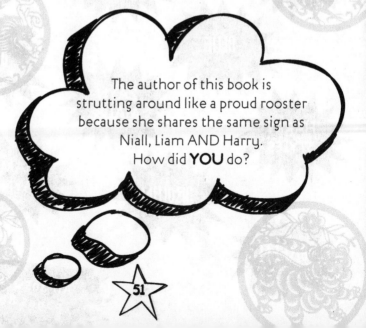

The author of this book is strutting around like a proud rooster because she shares the same sign as Niall, Liam AND Harry. How did **YOU** do?

THE EYES HAVE IT

Shut your eyes **NOW**. (Oh, hang on. Then you won't be able to read this. Hmm.) **OPEN** your eyes. But don't go peeking at any colour photos of **One Direction**, because this quiz is designed to test your memory. All you have to do is match the member of One Direction with the colour of their **eyes**. Easy, huh? ;-)

NIALL HORAN

BROWN

LOUIS TOMLINSON

BLUE

BLUE

ZAYN MALIK

HARRY STYLES

BROWN

LIAM PAYNE

GREEN

All answers on pages 88-93

Pup Direction – a group
of five talented dogs – once
performed a cover version of
One Direction's 'One Thing'.
It was called 'One Bark'.

TRUE FACT.

ONE DIRECTION HAVE BEEN
CALLED MANY THINGS.
BUT HERE ARE JUST A FEW OF THE
WAYS THEY'VE BEEN DESCRIBED.

1. THE FAMOUS FIVE

This is what **The Sunday Times** newspaper
called them. (It's also the name of a set of
characters created by Enid Blyton, who
starred in 21 books. Julian, Dick, Anne,
George and Timmy, the dog. Not many
people get them mixed up with One
Direction, though.)

2. THE FAB FIVE

The UK's Guardian NEWSPAPER called them
the Fab Five in homage to The Beatles, who were
known as the FAB FOUR. (Because there were four
of them and they were fab too, obviously.)

3. THE PRINCES OF POP

THIS IS WHAT **MTV** DUBBED THE BAND IN DECEMBER 2012. WHAT A ROYALLY FABULOUS NAME!

4. 1D

Probably the most famous **nickname** ever. **Seriously.** If there are extra-terrestrial life forms in the far reaches of space, they already know what 1D means.

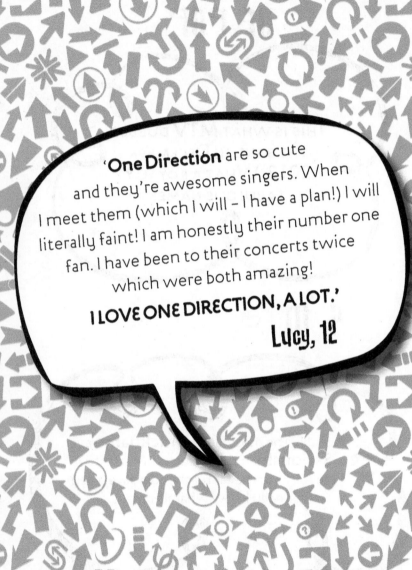

'**One Direction** are so cute and they're awesome singers. When I meet them (which I will – I have a plan!) I will literally faint! I am honestly their number one fan. I have been to their concerts twice which were both amazing!

I LOVE ONE DIRECTION, A LOT.'

Lucy, 12

☆ ☆ ☆ STUCK IN THE MIDDLE ☆ ☆ ☆

OK, SO YOU KNOW ALL OF THE BOYS' NAMES.
HOW ABOUT THEIR MIDDLE NAMES...? IS IT
HARRY HORATIO STYLES? OR MAYBE LOUIS
BERNARD TOMLINSON? ONLY JOKING..

Check out the list below and reunite each band member with their REAL middle name...

ZAYN MALIK

JAMES

NIALL HORAN

EDWARD

WILLIAM

LIAM PAYNE

HARRY STYLES

JAMES

JAVADD

LOUIS TOMLINSON

All answers on pages 88-93

The band members of **One Direction** are very loyal to their old mates from way back before they were famous, but that doesn't mean they don't have new celebrity BFFs too...

HARRY hangs out with BBC Radio 1 DJ NICK GRIMSHAW.

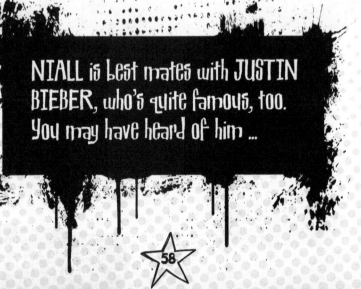

NIALL is best mates with JUSTIN BIEBER, who's quite famous, too. You may have heard of him ...

Did you know that **Ed Sheeran** wrote two tracks on One Direction's **Take Me Home** album? What you may not know is that after spending so much time recording **Little Things** and **Over Again** together, Ed is now one of **Harry's** celeb friends too.

Harry and **Alexandra Burke** (**The X Factor** winner 2008) are often photographed together. They get on so well, Harry was even invited to her last birthday party.

When **Michael Bublé** found out he was going to be a dad, one of the first people he told was his mate Niall!

BUT PERHAPS ONE DIRECTION'S MOST FAMOUS FRIENDS ARE … EACH OTHER. THEY REALLY DO GET ON, BIG TIME. AWWW. HOW COOL IS THAT?!

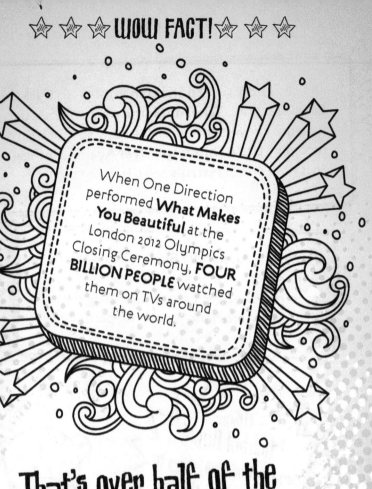

When One Direction performed **What Makes You Beautiful** at the London 2012 Olympics Closing Ceremony, **FOUR BILLION PEOPLE** watched them on TVs around the world.

That's over half of the world's population!

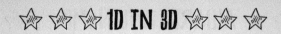
Films. Justin Bieber did it. Katy Perry did it, too. And then One Direction did it. Yay!

As if they weren't awesome enough in 2D, One Direction went one step further and in 2013 they starred in their very own 3D film!

To date, One Direction have been nominated for loads of awards and won a stack of them. Here are just a few...

2012

NOMINATED FOR FAVOURITE ALBUM, BAND AND NEW ARTIST OF THE YEAR AT THE AMERICAN MUSIC AWARDS.

WON Best International Artist at the Australian Recording Industry Association Music Awards (ARIA Music Awards).

WON Best British Album, Best British Music Act and Best British Single at the BBC Radio 1 Teen Awards.

WON the BRIT Award for Best British Single.

WON Best New Act, Best UK & Ireland Act and Biggest Fans at the MTV Europe Music Awards.

WON Best New Artist and Best Pop Video at the American MTV Video Music Awards.

WON the Global Success award at the BRIT Awards.

WON the Favourite Music Group and Favourite Song awards at the Nickelodeon Kids' Choice Awards.

One Direction once shared a photoshoot with some VERY beautiful Labrador puppies. The jury's out on whether it was the boys or the pups who were the most adorable. Whatever, it was furry good.

(Geddit? Furry good?! Sorry.)

BOTH LIAM AND HARRY HAD A CLOSE ENCOUNTER WITH A CUTE AND CUDDLY KOALA IN BRISBANE, AUSTRALIA. BUT THEY DIDN'T HAVE TO CLIMB A TREE TO MEET THE KOALA. ITS HOME WAS AN ANIMAL SANCTUARY.

 **Pet names**

All the One Direction boys have owned a pet at one time or another. Some have had a few. But here are the very first pets they owned.

Harry — a dog called Max

★★★★★

Liam — a terrapin called Frederick

★★★★★

Louis — a brown Labrador called Ted

★★★★★

Zayn — a dog called Tyson

★★★★★

Niall — two goldfish called Tom and Jerry

In January 2013, **One Direction** visited Ghana to see how donations made to the UK charity **Comic Relief** help families in urgent need of shelter, food and water. And even though they thought they knew what to expect, the boys were still stunned by the poverty they experienced. They were all moved to tears.

The African visit made One Direction even more keen to raise as much money as possible for Comic Relief, which meant saving money on the music video. Instead of splashing loads of cash, they got together with fans ...

and made the video themselves!

Did you know that One Direction's Comic Relief single was a cover version of not one but two 1970s hits? **One Way Or Another** was first recorded by US band Blondie and **Teenage Kicks** by the Undertones – both in 1978!

When tickets for One Direction's debut tour of the UK were released, they sold out in just **12 MINUTES.**

THE **ONE DIRECTION** BOYS HAVE HAD SOME
PRETTY FAMOUS GIRLFRIENDS, BUT WHICH OF
THE FOLLOWING HAVE THEY **NOT** DATED?

Leona Lewis

Madonna

Rihanna

Perrie Edwards

Rita Ora

Paloma Faith

Caroline Flack

Jessie J

Katy Perry

Taylor Swift

All answers on
pages 88-93

'Take Me Home marries sun-kissed US skater-pop with British charm.' BBC **review of One Direction's second album.**

'THEY came, they saw, they conquered. Dreams came true for thousands of Irish female fans as their pop idols One Direction took to the stage at the O2.' **Alexandra Ryan of Ireland's** *Evening Herald*, **after One Direction's sell-out gig at Dublin's The O2.**

'...the group that some people are saying are inspiring the next case of Beatlemania*...'
TV presenter on Today, **a US breakfast show.**

'The One Direction guys are great. We have a lot of fun whenever we hang out. They came over my house and we were just chilling out around the pool and listening to music.'
Justin Bieber

*Beatlemania happened in the 1960s when everyone fell in love with another band called The Beatles. Your grandparents will know ALL about them...

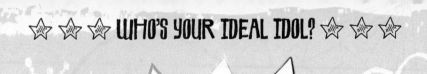

WHICH MEMBER OF ONE DIRECTION WOULD YOU get ALONG WITH BEST? ANSWER THESE MULTIPLE-CHOICE QUESTIONS TO FIND YOUR IDEAL ONE DIRECTION MATCH.

1. If you had a brand new pet, would you name it...?
a) Frederick
b) Tyson
c) Max
d) Ted
e) Tom. Or Jerry. Either one. Or both. You choose.

2. Is your favourite colour...?
a) blue
b) red
c) purple
d) orange

3. What quality do you most admire in a pop idol...?
a) vanity
b) common sense
c) leadership
d) cuteness
e) humour

4. If you had to pick another band you loved that WASN'T One Direction (yep, pretty difficult, huh?), would it be...?
a) The Fray
b) Coldplay
c) One Republic
d) The Script
e) *NSYNC

All answers on pages 88-93

HOW WELL DO YOU KNOW ONE DIRECTION?
TRY YOUR LUCK WITH THIS TOTALLY TRICKY TRIVIA QUIZ AND FIND OUT...

1. Were One Direction rescued from Heathrow Airport by ...?
a) A helicopter
b) A Batmobile
c) A police van
d) An ice-cream van

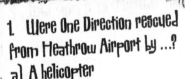

2. Which one of these nicknames have One Direction NOT been called ...?
a) The Fab Five
b) Boys Aloud
c) 1D
d) The Famous Five

3. Which of these singing sensations is BFFs with Niall?
a) Luciano Pavarotti
b) David Beckham
c) Justin Bieber
d) Britney Spears

4. The first band that two members of
One Direction ever went to see was Busted.
But which two?
 a) Louis and Niall
 b) Niall and Harry
 c) Harry and Zayn
 d) Zayn and Liam

5. Niall has a very strange phobia.
What does he really, really, REALLY not like?
 a) Ladders
 b) The number 13
 c) Spoons
 d) Forks

6. Who changed the spelling of their name
because they thought it looked better?
 a) Harri became Harry
 b) Luis became Louis
 c) Neil became Niall
 d) Zain became Zayn

All answers on
pages 88-93

✫ ✫ ✫ THE BIG QUIZ — PART I ✫ ✫ ✫

So, you've read the book and soaked up the facts.
How well do you know your idols now? Check out this
mega-quiz to find out if you're a true Directioner. There
are three parts to test your knowledge to the max.

1. WHICH MEMBER
of ONE DIRECTION WAS
TOO SHY TO MEET
HOLLYWOOD FILM STAR,
JOHNNY DEPP?

2. WHO TWEETED
ABOUT **THE QUEEN?**

3. WHO IS THE
ONLY IRISH MEMBER
OF THE BAND?

4. WHICH GUEST
JUDGE ON THE X FACTOR
SUGGESTED THAT THE
FIVE BOYS SHOULD SING
TOGETHER INSTEAD OF
SINGING SOLO?

5. WHO
THOUGHT OF THE
BAND'S NAME?

6. Whose pop idol is Robbie Williams?

7. Who owns turtles called Boris and Archimedes?

8. Who didn't have a passport before he joined One Direction?

10. Which US President's daughter is a fan of One Direction?

9. Who celebrates their birthday on Christmas Eve?

Were your answers FAN-tastic? Go to pages 88-93 to find out! And if you're up for a challenge, head to page 78 to take part II of THE BIG QUIZ. But beware – it's for true fans only...

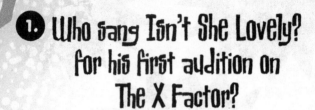

1. Who sang Isn't She Lovely? for his first audition on The X Factor?

2. Who's the youngest member of the band?

3. Who's the oldest member of the band?

4. Who's the shortest member of the band?

5. Whose favourite song is Thriller by Michael Jackson?

6. Where in Africa did One Direction go in January 2013 to find out about Comic Relief's fundraising efforts?

7. One Direction have been photographed with five Labradoodle puppies. True or false?

8. Which furry creature did Liam and Harry meet in Brisbane, Australia?

9. What was the name of Liam's terrapin?

10. Which member of One Direction is best mates with Michael Bublé?

All answers on pages 88-93

1. What did MTV call
One Direction?

2. Which fellow popstar
chilled out with
One Direction around his pool?

3. How many billion people
watched One Direction sing at
the London 2012 Olympic
Closing Ceremony?

4. Whose favourite song ever
is Shine On You Crazy Diamond
by Pink Floyd?

5. Which two bands first recorded
tracks that featured on One D's One
Way Or Another charity single for
Comic Relief?

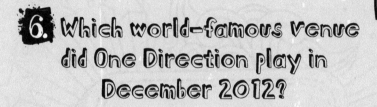

6. Which world-famous venue did One Direction play in December 2012?

7. Someone in One Direction has a mum called Tricia. Who?

8. Who suffered health problems with one of his kidneys for years?

9. Which band member can juggle?

10. What is One Direction's six-word slogan?

All answers on pages 88-93

☆ ☆ ☆ **WOW FACT!** ☆ ☆ ☆

ONE DIRECTION WERE FORMED AT **EXACTLY** 8.22PM ON FRIDAY 23 JULY 2010!

At the time of going to press, between them, the members of One Direction had a totally unbelievable 56,000,000 (that's FIFTY-SIX MILLION) Twitter followers.

Are you one of them?

HEROES (WITH **THE X FACTOR** FINALISTS 2010) – 21 NOVEMBER 2010

WHAT MAKES YOU BEAUTIFUL – 11 SEPTEMBER 2011

GOTTA BE YOU – 13 NOVEMBER 2011

WISHING ON A STAR (WITH **THE X FACTOR** FINALISTS 2011) – 27 NOVEMBER 2011

ONE THING – 12 FEBRUARY 2012

MORE THAN THIS – 25 MAY 2012

LIVE WHILE WE'RE YOUNG – 30 SEPTEMBER 2012

LITTLE THINGS – 11 NOVEMBER 2012

KISS YOU – 17 NOVEMBER 2012

ONE WAY OR ANOTHER (**TEENAGE KICKS**) – 17 FEBRUARY 2013

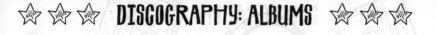

Up All Night – 21 November 2011

1. What Makes You Beautiful
2. Gotta Be You
3. One Thing
4. More Than This
5. Up All Night
6. I Wish
7. Tell Me a Lie
8. Taken
9. I Want
10. Everything About You
11. Same Mistakes
12. Save You Tonight
13. Stole My Heart

DISCOGRAPHY: ALBUMS

Take Me Home – 12 November 2012

1. Live While We're Young
2. Kiss You
3. Little Things
4. C'mon, C'mon
5. Last First Kiss
6. Heart Attack
7. Rock Me
8. Change My Mind
9. I Would
10. Over Again
11. Back For You
12. They Don't Know About Us
13. Summer Love

[Deluxe/ Yearbook/ BoxSet only]

14. She's Not Afraid
15. Loved You First
16. Nobody Compares
17. Still The One

WHAT'S NEXT FOR ONE DIRECTION?

They are the world's **BIGGEST** boy band.

They are **GLOBAL** superstars.

EVERYONE* has heard of them.

What's next for the **MIGHTY** One Direction? Who knows...? But **WHATEVER** it is, it's sure to be AWESOME.

*Everyone except someone with no TV and no newspapers and no magazines and no radio and no computer and no smartphone and no friends. So, um... pretty much everyone then.

PAGE 9
WHO SANG WHAT?

1. SO SICK
2. LET ME LOVE YOU
3. CRY ME A RIVER
4. ISN'T SHE LOVELY?
5. HEY THERE, DELILAH

PAGE 25
WHO'S WHO?

EARL JOHN ANIMALS = NIALL JAMES HORAN
JAVA LADY ADZ MINK = ZAYN JAVADD MALIK
MAILMAN SAY JEEP = LIAM JAMES PAYNE
DASTARDLY SHREW RYE = HARRY EDWARD STYLES
ILLUMINATION LIMO SLOWS = LOUIS WILLIAM
TOMLINSON

PAGE 37
SPOT THE SLOGAN

IT'S NUMBER 2. ONE BAND. ONE DREAM.
ONE DIRECTION.

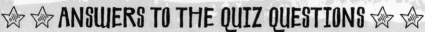

✩ ✩ ANSWERS TO THE QUIZ QUESTIONS ✩ ✩

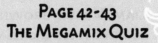

PAGE 42-43
THE MEGAMIX QUIZ

UNLOVELIER WEIGH YEW = LIVE WHILE WE'RE
YOUNG
FAT RISKS LISTS = LAST FIRST KISS
GONE THIN = ONE THING
NAP HUG TILL = UP ALL NIGHT
HAMLET OYSTER = STOLE MY HEART
TOGA BUY TOE = GOTTA BE YOU
HAIRNET MOTHS = MORE THAN THIS
THE TING TILLS = LITTLE THINGS
BOP DOO CARNMESY = NOBODY COMPARES
ARENA HERO NOW TOY = ONE WAY OR
ANOTHER

PAGE 45
WHO'S WHO?

THE VAIN ONE = ZAYN
THE SENSIBLE ONE = LIAM
THE LEADER = LOUIS
THE CUTE ONE = NIALL
THE FUNNY ONE = HARRY

PAGE 52
THE EYES HAVE IT

NIALL HORAN = BLUE
ZAYN MALIK = BROWN

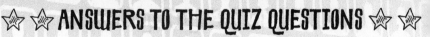

LIAM PAYNE = BROWN
HARRY STYLES = GREEN
LOUIS TOMLINSON = BLUE

PAGE 57
STUCK IN THE MIDDLE

NIALL HORAN = JAMES
ZAYN MALIK = JAVADD
LIAM PAYNE = JAMES
HARRY STYLES = EDWARD
LOUIS TOMLINSON = WILLIAM

PAGE 69
GIRLFRIENDS

(ACTUAL AND RUMOURED GIRLFRIENDS)
TAYLOR SWIFT
LEONA LEWIS
PERRIE EDWARDS
CAROLINE FLACK

(NOT GIRLFRIENDS)
KATY PERRY
RIHANNA
JESSIE J
PALOMA FAITH
RITA ORA
MADONNA

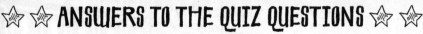

☆ ☆ ANSWERS TO THE QUIZ QUESTIONS ☆ ☆

PAGE 72-73
WHO'S YOUR IDEAL IDOL?

1 A. FREDERICK (LIAM)
B. TYSON (ZAYN)
C. MAX (HARRY)
D. TED (LOUIS)
E. TOM OR JERRY (NIALL)

2 A. BLUE (NIALL)
B. RED (ZAYN OR LOUIS)
C. PURPLE (LIAM)
D. ORANGE (HARRY)

3 A. VANITY (ZAYN)
B. COMMON SENSE (LIAM)
C. LEADERSHIP (LOUIS)
D. CUTENESS (NIALL)
E. HUMOUR (HARRY)

4 A. THE FRAY (LOUIS)
B. COLDPLAY (HARRY)
C. ONE REPUBLIC (LIAM)
D. THE SCRIPT (NIALL)
E. *NSYNC (ZAYN)

Page 74-75
Top Trivia Quiz

1. C - a police van
2. B - Boys Aloud
3. C - Justin Bieber
4. A - Louis and Niall
5. C - spoons
6. D - Zain became Zayn

Page 76-77
The Big Quiz - Part 1

1. Zayn
2. Harry
3. Niall
4. Nicole Scherzinger
5. Harry
6. Louis
7. Liam
8. Zayn
9. Louis
10. Barack Obama

Page 78-79
The Big Quiz - Part II

1. Harry
2. Harry
3. Louis
4. Niall
5. Zayn
6. Ghana
7. False. They were labradors
8. Koala
9. Frederick
10. Niall

Page 80-81
The Big Quiz - Part III

1. The Princes of Pop
2. Justin Bieber
3. Four billion
4. Harry
5. Blondie & The Undertones
6. Madison Square Garden
7. Zayn
8. Liam
9. Harry
10. One band. One dream. One direction.

☆ ☆ ☆ INDEX ☆ ☆ ☆

Congratulations!

Now you really, truly **KNOW** your idols (probably better than their own mums). But what about your **OTHER** idols, like **Katy Perry**, **Olly Murs**, **Robert Pattinson** and **James Arthur**?

WHAT ABOUT THEM...?

DON'T PANIC.

Simply check out the other titles in the series and become an

EVEN BIGGER FAN.

Want to Know Your Idol?

TOTALLY AWESOME TITLES IN THE SERIES:

9780750279321

9780750279338

9780750279307

9780750279314

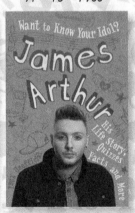

9780750278386

9780750278362

WHY NOT COLLECT THEM ALL?

96